Apple Watch Series 8 2022 Beginners Guide

A Simple Manual to Help You Navigate the Apple Watch Series 8, Watch Se, And Ultra: With Step-by-Step Tutorials, Tips and Tricks for WatchOS 9

D1525648

Jeremy Lawson

Table of content

What's New to Apple Watch 8 And Watch Os9

By popular demand the Apple Watch 8 has been announced for September 2022. This latest version of the Apple Watch series which was originally launches in 2015 is not much different from its predecessor, Apple Watch 7 series.

Materials and Colours

The Watch 8 series has two versions, which are aluminum models and stainless-steel models. The former is available in RED, STARLIGHT, MIDNIGHT, & SILVER while the latter is available in GRAPHITE GOLD AND SILVER.

Design and Functionality

The Apple 8 series doesn't offer much updates in terms design and functionality compared to older models like series 7 or 6. It features the same size options (41mm - 45mm), slim-bordered display, sapphire crystal backing, round-edged casings, faster charging speed and Digital Crown with tactile feedback as the Apple 7 series.

The embedded chip 8 is similar to that of the Watch Series 6 which was launched in 2020, the speed stays unchanged. To be fair, the watch 8 series has some unique features which include an inbuilt temperature sensor, undergoes temperature reading per 5 seconds which enables it to detect even the slightest change in temperature.

One of the most iconic features of the Apple Watch 8 is a new Crash Detection feature. That is, you Apple Watch 8 is programmed to detect serious car crashes and immediately contact the emergency services.

Battery Life

The battery life is still unchanged as that of the earlier Watch series 7 but can be prolonged to a maximum of 36 hours with the newly introduced Low Power Mode. Meanwhile, this power mode disables heart rate measurement, Always-On Display, limits cellular connection and WIFI range among other things.

Workout Enhancement

Apple watch 8 enhances your workout regime by giving insights into the best exercise forms in order to use your time effectively.

Reminders for Medications and sleeping pattern

The new Watch 8 series has unique feature that aids in entering medication schedule. Once, this information has been logged into your watch, it automatically sends Medications. This device also provide estimates the time range spent on the various sleep stages.

Finally, Apple Watch buyers can look forward to International Roaming which enables the Watch to maintain their cellular plans even while travelling anywhere in the world

Chapter One

Pairing And Setting Your Apple Watch

Using your iPhone to start and pair your watch, make sure your mobile phone is updated to the most recent version of IOS linked to a Wi-Fi or cellular network and has got Bluetooth turned on. It is important to make sure that the iPhone device and watch are close to each other during the entire set up process.

Pair Apple Watch with iPhone

First, switch on the series 8, then click and hold onto the side button to switch it on. Then unlock your iPhone and place it close to your watch until a message pop up, and press continue on your mobile phone.

After that, press set up for myself. Point your iPhone camera at the animation on the Watch 8. But if you cannot make use of the camera, then press pair it on your watch manually on your iPhone and adhere to the guide.

Then, look out for a message that tells you that your apple watch is paired.

How To Set Up Your Apple Watch

When getting started, press set up apple watch, then strictly adhere to the guidelines on your Watch 8 device and iPhone to complete set up.

Charge The Apple Watch

To charge the apple watch, place the charger or charging cable on a flat surface, then plug the charger into a power adapter. Also plug the adapter into a power outlet.

Watch Gestures

The Watch 8 has got several gestures used in interacting with it. These gestures include tapping, swiping and dragging with a finger.

Trouble Pairing

There are number of ways of fixing the connection if your Watch 8 has issues pairing with your iPhone device. A red iPhone image is displayed at the top of the display in your Watch 8 if it's not pairing, this is caused as a result of your iPhone being too far from your smartwatch. To resolve this, the Watch 8 needs to be brought close to your iPhone because the phone and the watch pair via Bluetooth.

Another trouble that may arise during pairing might be from your setting. Check the settings of your watch and phone, if your phone has its Bluetooth turned off or either of the devices are in airplane mode, they won't be able to pair up. Make sure all settings reset properly to facilitate the connection.

If trying all these methods doesn't resolve the connection, try restarting the devices (iPhone and watch). You may equally try resetting the network connection on your iPhone. If resetting your network connection doesn't resolve the pairing issue, try reset your watch.

Apple Watch Family Set Up

For a person who does not own an iPhone, for example a child in Elementary school or a parent, you can set up and manage apple watch. Creating an Apple series watch for your family is same as creating a watch for yourself. After switching on the series 8, put your iPhone and your watch side by side, then watch out for your Watch 8 screen that you will use for pairing to display on your iPhone, after that, click continue to proceed. Next, tap set up for a family member, then click on continue. Place your iPhone in order for the series 8 shows in the view finder in the series 8 application. This pairs both devices. Then press set up apple watch. Adhere to the guidelines on your series 8 and iPhone to finish set up.

School Time On Apple Watch

A member of the family stays focus during school period by limiting the features on your Watch 8.

Basic Things You Need to Know

The Apple Watch Application: In your iPhone, the Watch 8 application is used to install apps, configure the dock, adjust settings and notifications, etc. For you to access the watch app, you have to switch on your iPhone, press the Watch 8 application icon. Click My Watch to view the settings for your

Watch 8 If your iPhone is paired with more than one apple watch, you view your active apple watch settings.

Switch On and Wake Your Watch 8: To switch on your Watch 8 when off, click and hold the side button till the apple symbol appear.

Always On:

The Always On in your watch displays the watch time and face. When the power mode is low on your Watch 8, the Always On is off. To see the watch face, press the display.

Wake Up the Apple Watch Screen

The Watch 8 screen can be woken up by raising your wrist, or tapping the digital crown, and turning the digital crown upward. To switch off the wake up on the series 8, visit your settings, tap turn off wake on your watch and press display.

Go Back to Clock Face

One can know the duration which the Watch 8 return to it clock face from an open application by simply opening the setting application on the series 8. Visit general, go back to clock and scroll down and select the time you want your series 8 to return to clock face. It could be after 3 minutes, 5 minutes, 10 minutes or Always, depending on the one you prefer. You can return to clock faces through the digital crown.

Wake Up Last Activity

In certain applications, the Watch 8 can be set to return to where you were before it went to sleep. This is done by opening the setting application on your Watch 8. Visit general, go back to to clock, move down and press an application, then switch on return to app.

Leave Your Apple Watch Screen on For a Long Period Of Time

 The Watch 8 screen can be kept on for a long period of time by opening the setting application on your watch. Click on display and brightness, then press wake duration and press wake for 70 seconds.

Lock Or Unlock Your Apple Watch

The Watch 8 can be locked and unlocked automatically and manually. The apple watch locks automatically when it is off your wrist. By holding the downside of the display and swiping up to enter control center, it locks manually. Tap ⬚ and your Watch 8 locks. The Watch 8 can be unlocked manually by entering your passcode and can also be unlocked immediately when you open your iPhone

Change Watch Passcode

Your iPhone can change the passcode on your series 8 by unpairing your watch with your iPhone to delete your Watch 8 settings and passcode. This happens when you want to re-setup your series 8 and have it paired with your device.

Turn Off the Passcode

To switch off the passcode on your series 8, go to setting application on your watch, then press passcode, then press turn off passcode.

Erase Apple Watch Automatically

To erase series 8, open your settings in your watch series, press passcode, then switch on erase data.

Change Language/Region

You can select the language that appears on your Watch 8 if you have configured your iPhone to use more than one language. Go to your Watch 8 application on your iPhone. Press My Watch, visit General, then proceed to region and language, press custom, and select a language.

Change Wrist Orientation or Digital Crown

Your wrist orientation can be changed on your apple Watch by adjusting the settings of your orientation so that when you lift your wrist, it wakes your apple watch series, which enables switching the Digital Crown navigation of things in the way you want it to be.

Watch apps

There are various applications in the watch series. These includes Audiobook, Calculator, Mindfulness, Podcasts, Reminders, Phone, Photos, Stock, Walkie-Talkie, Weather, Workout, Apple Pay Alarms and so on.

Organizing Your Apps

How To Open Your App

You can access your watch series through the home menu screen in your Apple watch series. The Dock in your

Watch 8 gives you immediate access to your applications you used the most.

Arrange Your Apps

Your apps on the home screen in your Apple watch are arranged in a grid and list view. To choose any of the view, click and hold onto the home display. Select list or grid view.

Open An App from Your Home Screen

To visit an app from your home screen depends on the angle you choose. If you choose the Grid angle, switching the Digital Crown enables leads you to opening the app which is in the middle point of the visuals, but for the list view, you will have to turn the Digital Crown, then press an app.

Open Apps from The Dock

Press the button at the top side/angle of the watch series then switch the digital crown to navigate throughout the applications in your docks. Press an app to it.

Remove an App from Your Apple Watch

To remove an application from your Watch 8, in a grid view, you need to touch and hold onto the home display, press edit apps, then to remove the application, tap the X. Swiping the application in an enabled list-like view, to the left, then tap the delete icon to delete it from your watch is something you can do.

Adjust App Settings

To adjust an app in your watch 8, simply open your Apple series app on your iPhone. The next thing to do is the click on My Watch, after that, navigate through the screen to view the installed apps. Click on your desired app to modify it settings.

Getting More Applications on Your Apple Series 8

Getting more applications on your Apple series 8 can simply be done when you, open your App store, then switch your digital crown in order to browse featured apps. Next, click on, See All option, which is below a collection, this will enable you to see multiple apps.

Download from App Store

To download from the store, tap Get to receive a free application and to buy an app tap the price

Install Apps That Are Already in Your iPhone

If you have got the Apple series Watch application installed in your device, it will automatically make your device apps to be installed in your apple series. If you decide to install specific app, open up the apple series app which is on your device. My Watch is what you should click on first, then press General, then switch off the automatic application, install. Click on My Watch and move down to see all the apps available for your use. Press install close to the applications that you desire to install.

Tell The Time on Your Apple Watch

The Apple series Watch has got four different ways of telling the time. Firstly, by raising your wrist. The time displays in the clock in grid view. Secondly, by hearing the time. You could listen to the time by switching on your Speak Time in your clock in your settings app. Thirdly, by feeling the timer. You could see the time by switching on the taptic time in your clock in your settings app. Fourthly, you can use Siri. Check on your wrist, then tell me the time.

Apple Series Watch Status Icon

The apple series 8 has got status icon which is found at the kingpin bar of your screen. The status icon gives you knowledge about your apple series 8. Some of these are the status icons and what they mean.

Status Icon Meaning

The red circular shape indicates you have an unread message, and you need to swipe down in your watch to view it.

The green S indicates the Apple Watch is charging.

The red S indicates that the Apple series Watch battery is low.

The yellow circular shape shows that the low power mode is on.

The purple half moon tells you that Do Not Disturb is switched on. You will not be notified on your alerts and calls, neither will it light up.

The padlock symbol represents your Apple series 8, it is locked and has to be unlock by entering your passcode.

The airplane icon on the screen displayed on your series watch represents your airplane mode, which is switched on.

The red X indicates that the Watch 8 with cellular lost its cellular connection.

.

Using Control Center on Apple Watch 8

The control center in your Apple series 8 makes it easy to access your battery, turn on flashlight in your series watch, select a focus, switch on your airplane icon, heater mode etc.

Open Or Close Control Center

Opening of control center: In the series Face, click on Swipe up. But from other screen click and hold onto the button of your screen, then swipe up.

Close Control Center: Swipe down from the top of the screen or click on the digital crown

Switch On Your Airplane Mode

To switch on airplane mode, swipe up to the open up the control center then click on and your airplane mode is switched on. When the airplane icon is switched on, it turns off the Wi-Fi and cellular and keeps the Bluetooth switched on.

Use The Apple Watch Flashlight

To switch on the flashlight in your Apple series, swipe up to your control center, then click on it. You can select a mode by swiping left.

To switch off the flashlight in your Apple series, swipe below from the top of the series face or click on the side button or Digital Crown. The flashlight is used to light up a dark area.

Theatre Mode

The theater mode can be activated on your Apple series when you swipe up to open up the control center. Then, go ahead and tap the theater mode. The theater mode prevents the Apple series visuals from switching on when you have raised your wrist.

Disconnect From Wi- Fi

To disconnect your Watch from Wi-Fi, then swipe to open up the control arena and click on Wi-Fi in the control center and your Apple series disconnect from Wi-Fi.

Turn On Silent Mode

You can turn on your silent mode by swiping up to enter the control center, then click silent □

Find Your iPhone

If ever your device is nearby, your Apple series Watch can help you locate it. You swipe up to open the control arena and tap ☐. After that, your device will make a sound so that you can locate it.

Find Your Apple Watch

When you can't find your watch, you can use the Find My app on your device and iCloud to locate your Apple series.

Connecting To Wi- Fi

You can connect your Watch 8 to a Wi-Fi by swiping up to enter the control center. Touch and hold onto the Wi-Fi, then click the accessible Wi- Fi network. Wi- Fi networks that matches Watch 8 are 802.11b/g/n 2.4GHz.

Monitor Headphone Volume

To monitor the headphones volume in your Apple series Watch, swipe up to enter the control center. Tap □ to monitor your headphone volume. A meter shows the current headphone volume.

Chapter Two

Adjust Brightness and Text Size

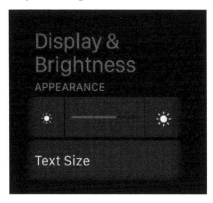

To adjust the brightness and text size, open the setting app on your Apple series Watch, then press the display and brightness to adjust the brightness. To adjust text size, tap text size, then tap the letters or turn the Digital Crown.

Adjust The Sound

To adjust the sound, visit the settings app in your watch 8. Click on sound and haptics. Tap the volume control under alert volume

Adjust Haptic Intensity

To adjust haptic intensity, go to settings app on your watch. Click sound and haptics, then switch on haptic alert

Turn Digital Crown Haptics Off or On

To turn the digital crown haptics off or on in your Apple Watch, go to your settings app on your Watch and tap the Haptics and Sound, then turn Crown Haptics off or on

Use Taptic Time

When the Watch 8 is in silent mode, The Taptic time taps out time on your wrist with a series of different tap. To turn on the Taptic time, go to your settings application in your Watch 8. Click on

Clock, and scroll down, then tap Taptic time to switch it on.

See And Respond to Notifications on Your Apple Watch

This is done by swiping down to open the notification center. Swipe up or down or switch the Digital Crown which scrolls the notification list. Then click the notification to read or respond to it.

Apple Id Settings

The Apple ID settings helps you see and edit data that connects to your Apple ID. You can include and edit your contact info, reset your password, and more.

Change Your Contact Information

To change your contact info, go to settings application on your Watch 8. Click your username. Then click Name, Phone number, E-mail, then do one of the following

Manage Apple ID Password and Security

You can manage your security and Apple ID password by opening the settings app on your Apple series Watch. Tap Your Username. Then click password and security, then do any of the following.

View and Manage Subscriptions

You can view and manage subscription by clicking on Your Username after opening the Setting app. Click subscription, tap a subscription to view information about it. To end subscription, you can press Cancel

Using Shortcut

The shortcut is an application on your device that allows you trigger task with just a tap. The shortcut could be run on the shortcut application or include them as complications to your watch face.

Run A Shortcut

For you to run a shortcut, open the shortcut application on your Watch 8 and choose a shortcut.

Add A Shortcut Complication

Touch and hold onto the watch face, then click Edit. Swipe left to the complication display, then click a complication. Scroll to shortcut and select a shortcut.

Add More Shortcut to Apple Watch

To add more shortcut to Apple Watch, you need to visit the shortcut application on your iphone. Click ••• in the top right corner of a shortcut. Tap i on the shortcut screen and switch on Show on Apple Watch.

Create An Emergency Medical ID Card

A Medical ID offers data about you which could be vital in an urgent situation like allergies and medical issues Your iPhone and Watch 8 can show the info.

Set Up Your Medical ID

Go to the health app on your iPhone, to set up your medical ID. First tap your profile picture at the top right, then press medical ID. Press Get Started or Edit, then input your info. Add emergency contact and your contact number. Then tap Done.

View Your Medical ID

To view your medical ID from the Home Screen, tap the health app icon, then choose medical ID

Set Up Handwashing on Your Apple Watch

To setup handwashing on your Apple series Watch notify you if you haven't washed within a few minutes of going back home. Your Apple series Watch detects when you have started washing and motivates you to continue for 20 seconds, the time suggested by global health organization.

Switch On Handwashing

To switch on handwashing, go to the settings area on your Apple series Watch and click on handwashing and switch on handwashing timer.

Receive Handwashing Alert

You get handwashing alert by opening the settings application on your series 8. Click on handwashing and switch on handwashing reminders.

Chapter Three

Measure Blood Oxygen Levels on Apple Watch

Use Blood Oxygen application on your Apple series Watch 8 to know how much oxygen your red blood cells takes from your lungs to the rest of your body. This helps general health and fitness can be better understood by understanding how well circulated your blood is.

Unfortunately, not every region has access to the Blood Oxygen app. Readings from blood oxygen apps are not meant for healthcare purpose.

Set Up Blood Oxygen

On your Apple Watch, launch the Settings application. Switch on Blood Oxygen Readings by tapping Blood Oxygen.

It is important to disable background measurements, when the Sleep Focus or Theater Mode.

A red light that is always bright is used to assess your blood oxygen levels and glows against your wrist; this light may very well be easier to see in dimly lit areas. If the light distracts you in the course of your readings, you can switch it off. On your Apple Watch, launch the Settings application. After selecting Blood Oxygen, switch off Theater Mode and Sleep Focus.

Measure Your Blood Oxygen Level

If background readings are enabled, the Blood Oxygen application will regularly check your blood oxygen condition during daytime, but you can also take an on-demand reading at any moment. On your Watch 8 launch the Blood Oxygen application. Place your wrist flat, watch 8 displays facing up, and place your arm on a desk or in your lap. During the 15-second wait, hold your arm perfectly motionless after selecting Start. You are given the findings following the assessment. Click Done.

Please take note: It is important to note that your Apple Watch's rear requires skin contact. Effective blood oxygen readings are increased if your

Apple Watch is worn comfortably, without being too stiff or free and with enough space for your body to be able to breathe.

Record An Electrocardiogram with The ECG App

Upgrade your iPhone 8 or the most recent iOS release and your Apple Watch to the most recent version of watchOS in order to use the ECG application. On Apple Watch 8 and in some regions, the ECG app is not accessible. Launch the Health app on your iPhone, then set up ECG by following the instructions on the screen. If you don't see a setup prompt, click Browse in the down right corner, select

Heart, and select Electrocardiogram (ECG).

Open the ECG App on Your Apple Watch.

It is important for your arm should be at your side or on a table. Hold your finger on the Digital Crown with the hand facing your watch, and then see the Apple Watch captures the ECG.

You are given a categorization at the conclusion of the recording. The next step is to select Add Symptoms and select the symptoms you have. To record any symptoms, hit Save, then tap Done. Launch the Health app on your iPhone, press Browse in the down right, then select Heart > Electrocardiograms to examine your findings (ECG).

Useful Tip: After swimming, taking a shower, perspiring heavily, or cleaning your hands, thoroughly dry and clean, use your Apple Watch to get the finest reading. Your Apple Watch might need an additional hour or more to dry completely. ECG is intended to operate between 0° and 35° C and 32° and 95° F.

Use Calculator on Apple Watch

It is interesting to know that your Apple Watch can help you carry out simple arithmetic calculations with the Calculator app. You can divide the check and immediately figure out the tip.

For instance, using Siri, you can ask a simple question like "What is 5×3" or "What percentage of 225 is 18?"

Perform a Quick Calculation

Get your Apple Watch and launch the Calculator app. To get a result, tap operators and numbers.

Divide the check in half and add a tip.

Get your Apple Watch and launch the Calculator app. Then, click Tip after entering the total sum of the bill. It is necessary to turn the Digital Crown, select a tip percent. To input the number of persons splitting the bill, click People and then switch the Digital Crown. If the bill is divided equally, you may see the tip amount, the overall cost, and how much each customer owes.

Calendar

Your Apple Watch's Calendar app displays events you have booked or been called to for the last six weeks as well as the next two years (in List and Day view). Events from all of your iPhone's calendars or simply the calendars you select are displayed on your Apple Watch. For instructions on configuring the Calendar app on your iPhone, consult the iPhone User Guide.

Making use of Siri, you can ask something along the lines of "When is my next occasion?"

See Calendar Events

Tap an event or date on the watch face to access the Calendar application on your Watch 8. The Digital Crown may be switched to check future events. To view information about an event, like the time, place, invitee standing, and notes, click on it.

Change How You View Events

Access the Calendar application on your Apple Watch, select the More icon, and then click an option to change views. Displays your future events for the week under Up Next. Day: Displays only the activities for this day.

List: Displays every event you have from the previous two weeks to the following two years. If you're in Day view, slide left or right; if you are in Up Next view or List View, switch the Digital Crown to see another day. Select the present time in the top-right corner of the screen to return to the present day and time.

View Weeks And Months

You can switch between week and month views while perusing events in Day or List view. Choose one of the actions after opening the Calendar application on your Watch 8:

To show activities for a specific week, on the weekly calendar, tap a day.

Displaying the current month: Click the top-left arrow when the current week is displayed.

Another month to display: Digital Crown turned.

In the monthly calendar and select the week.

Add An Event

Events you add to the iPhone's Calendar app are automatically linked with your Apple Watch. Activities can also be created directly from your watch.

Using Siri, create a FaceTime with Mom calendar event for June 11 at 2 p.m., for example.

Utilize the Calendar application on your Watch 8 by tapping the More button while you are browsing events in Up Next, Day, or List mode, then selecting New Event. Select the calendar you want to add the event to, enter the event's name, summary, date, and time, and invited guests, then click Add.

A fresh event is displayed on the calendar. The event's title is at the top, and a field for the location is below. An All-day button is located close to the bottom. A Start Date button is located at the bottom.

To erase an event, you planned: Select an event, hit Delete, then hit Delete once more. If it is a regular event, you can choose to eliminate just this particular event or all upcoming ones. Modify a happening: Utilize the iPhone's Calendar app.

Respond to a Calendar Invitation

Event invitations can be replied to on your Watch 8 immediately or later.

Upon receiving the invitation, if you see it: Select Accept, Decline, or Perhaps at the bottom of the message after scrolling to the bottom.

If you later learn about the notification: In the menu of notifications, click it, then scroll and reply.

If the Calendar application is already open: To react, tap the occasion. Press the name of the event planner in the event information, click the phone, messaging, Walkie-Talkie or email buttons to get in touch with them.

Get Directions to an Event

You can get directions to an event using Apple Watch. Get your Watch's Calendar app open. After tapping an event, tap the location.

Change "Leave Now" Alerts

If an event has a place, your Apple Watch will immediately send you a "leave now" notice depending on the anticipated time it will take you to get there and the current traffic situation. Do the following to select a certain time window, such two hours before the event.

Launch The iPhone's Calendar App

Hit the occasion. Then select a new interval by tapping Alert.

Adjust Calendar Settings

You can choose which calendars will show up on your Apple Watch and alter the types of calendar messages you get by doing the following:

On your iPhone, launch the Apple Watch app. Click Calendar after tapping My Watch. Under Calendars or notifications select Custom.

Chapter Four

Use Camera Remote and Timer on Apple Watch

You can make use of your Watch 8 to check the camera of your iPhone and snap the shot if you wish to place your iPhone for a photo and take it from a range. In order to drop your wrist and lift your gaze when you are in the picture; a shutter timer can also be established using the Watch 8.

It is important for your Watch 8 to be within typical Bluetooth distance of your iPhone in order to work as a camera remote (about 33 feet or 10 meters).

Say words like Take a photo," Siri.

Take a Photo

On your Apple Watch, launch the Camera Remote application. By utilizing your Apple Watch as a viewfinder, place your iPhone to compose the photo.

Switch the Digital Crown to zoom. To change exposure, click the shot's focal point in the Apple Watch preview. Click the Shutter button to take the picture. You can see the image on your Apple Watch after it has been taken and stored in Images on your iPhone.

Review Your Shots

The actions listed below can be used for photos reviews on your Watch 8.

See a picture: In the down left corner, tap the thumbnail.

View more images: swipe left or right.

the entire screen Select the image twice.

To show or conceal the shot count and the Close button, tap the display.

Tap Close when you're finished.

Use the Compass App on Apple Watch

The Compass app's Compass symbol displays your actual location, height, and the route your Apple Watch 8 is. You may construct Compass Waypoints on the Apple Watch SE and Apple Watch Series 6 and later, find the direction and distance between them, and utilize Backtrack to reverse your movements.

It should be noted that removing the Compass software from your iPhone also removes it from your Watch.

On the watch face, the middle displays your bearing. Your slope, elevation, and positions are displayed in the inner ring of the compass as you scroll the digital crown. To display the locations of the waypoints you set, keep scrolling.

Open the Compass App the Compass Icon

You can add a bearing by tapping the List button, scrolling down to Bearing, selecting the bearing, and then tapping Done.

The bearing can be changed by tapping the List button, scrolling down to Bearing, selecting the new bearing, and then tapping Done.

Hit the List button, scroll down, select Clear Bearing, and then tap Done to remove the bearing.

Note: Not all regions may have coordinates accessible.

Create and Display Compass Waypoints

The Compass app on an Apple Watch 8 allows you to add your exact location as a waypoint. The distance and direction to each Compass Waypoint you establish are then visible.

On your Watch, press the Compass icon to launch the Compass app.

To add a waypoint, use the Waypoint button.

Tap Done after entering the waypoint's label, color, or symbol (such as "vehicle" or "home"). Hit a waypoint on any of the three Compass screens, use the Digital Crown to choose a waypoint, then click Select to view a Compass Waypoint. The waypoint's location and direction are displayed on the screen, such as "3.7 miles to your left."

The waypoint and its locations will appear on a map when you tap the bottom of the screen. Tap the Edit button on the waypoint screen to change the information for the currently chosen waypoint. The waypoint editing panel in the Compass app. At the very top is the Label field. There is a Location box below that displays the waypoint's coordinates on a map. The waypoint has been marked with the dining symbol.

Add Compass Waypoint Complications to The Watch Face

You can easily find your parked car, the last waypoint you viewed in the Compass app, or waypoints you've established with the aid of a Compass Waypoint complication.

Press and hold onto the screen when the watch face is visible and hit Edit.

Up until the very end, swipe left. The final screen displays any issues that a face may provide. Toggle the Digital Crown to Compass Waypoints, tap a complication to choose it, and then choose from the options below.

To include a waypoint as a complication, tap one of the first three listed waypoints. Click More, select a waypoint, the most recent waypoint you saw, or the parked car waypoint. Tap the face to switch to it after pressing the Digital Crown to save your changes.

Maps

Get Info About a Landmark or Marked Location

Touch the location marker on your map. To view the information, switch the Digital Crown. To continue to the map, click or slide in the upper-left corner.

Drop, move, and remove map pins

Drop a pin: When the pin has dropped the place you want it to, release your hold on the map after waiting for a moment.

Touch the blue dot, then select Mark My Location to put a pin where you are right now.

Move a pin: Drag the pin by touching and holding it, then drop another pin in the new spot.

The Maps app displays a map with a red pin on it that can be utilized as an endpoint for instructions or to acquire an approximation of an address for a location on the map.

Get Directions

Get your Apple Watch's Maps app open. To navigate to Favorites, Guides, and Recents, turn the Digital Crown. To get driving, pedestrian, transit, and bicycle instructions, touch an entry.

Not all forms of transportation are accessible everywhere.

After which, click a pathway to start your journey and see a summary of it with turns, distances between turns, and street names. Click a mode to see recommended routes.

You may find your expected arrival time by looking in the upper-left corner. To find out how long it will take you to get there, tap the arrival time.

See Transportation Options

In the Maps app, proposed routes are displayed, allowing you to choose several possibilities before setting out.

If an alternative path appears, select it by tapping on it.

Change to a route that involves cycling, walking, transit, or driving: Select Cycling, Transit, Walking, or Driving.

Avoid tolls and motorways by selecting > next to the location's address and turning on an option when a driving route is displayed.

Avoid hills and congested roads: When a bike route is displayed, select an alternative by tapping > next to the destination's address.

Select your preferred mode of public transportation: When a route for your preferred mode of transportation is displayed, tap >. Then, select your desired mode from the list, such as bus, commuter rail, light rail, or ferry.

Get Directions to a Landmark or Map Pin

Get your Apple Watch's Maps app open. Then, tap the location's landmark or map point by tapping Location. Select walking, driving, taking public transportation, or cycling routes after scrolling the location data until you see Directions. Select a route when you are prepared to go, then adhere to the instructions.

Siri: Asking how long it will take you to get home is a good example.

Use Maps while enroute

You can stay on the correct road with a variety of features on your Apple Watch. As you travel, pick one of these:

View turn-by-turn directions: As soon as your trip is underway, Apple Watch lists all the turns you'll make, including street and highway names. To view upcoming turns, switch the Digital Crown. To revert back to the next turn you'll take, click the top of the display.

Turn-by-turn directions cannot be used until location services are enabled. To enable or disable location services on Apple Watch, navigate to Settings > Privacy & Security > Location Services.

View a map: To see a map that displays the location of each turn in a list of turn-by-turn directions, hit the Map button. Zoom in and out on the map by using the Digital Crown. To revert to the turn-by-turn list, click the List button.

Pay attention to the signs: Your Apple Watch employs touches and to signal when to switch once you start your first leg. At the crossroads you are reaching, turn right if you hear a low tone resulting in a high tone, and turn left if you hear a high tone accompanied by a low tone (tick tock, tick tock). Uncertain of how your destination will appear? When you're on the last leg or when you get there, you'll feel a vibration.

The kinds of transportation that offer warnings are your choice. Switch on the notifications you want to get for Walking, Cycling, Driving and Driving with CarPlay by opening the Apple Watch app on your iPhone, tapping My Watch, and then tapping Maps.

Track Your Sleep with Apple Watch

You may make bedtime plans with the Sleep app on Apple Watch to help you achieve your sleep objectives. Wear your watch to bed, and Apple Watch can predict when you might have woken up as well as how much time you spent in each stage of sleep (REM, Core, and Deep). Open the Sleep app when you wake up to discover how much sleep you received and your sleep patterns over the previous 14 days.

You are reminded to charge your Apple Watch if it is less than 30% recharged before night. Simply take a quick look at the welcome in the morning to determine how much charge is left.

You can make different timetables, such as one for the weekdays and another for the weekends.

Set up Sleep on Apple Watch

Get your Watch 8 and launch the Sleep app.

Obey the directions displayed on the screen.

On the iPhone, launch the Health app, select Browse, select Sleep, and then select Get Started (under Set Up Sleep).

Alter or disable your subsequent wake-up alarm

Get your Apple Watch and launch the Sleep app.

Your present bedtime will appear.

Hit the wake-up time, move the Digital Crown to another time, and then select the Check button to establish a new wake-up time.

Turn off Alarm if you don't want your Apple Watch to wake you up in the morning.

To modify your plan, launch the Health application on your iPhone, press Browse, hit Sleep, and then touch Edit next to Your Schedule.

Only your subsequent wake-up alarm will be affected; thereafter, your regular schedule will operate.

Remarkably, you can disable the subsequent wake-up alarm in the Alarms app. Simply select Skip for Tonight after tapping the alarm that displays under Sleep | Wake up.

Change or Add a Sleep Schedule

Get your Apple Watch and launch the Sleep app.

Toggle Full Schedule, then choose from one of these:

Click the current schedule to make changes to it.

Tap Add Schedule to add a sleep schedule.

Modify your sleep target: Set your desired amount of sleep time by tapping Sleep Goal.

Adjust the amount of time the Wind Down feature is active by tapping Wind Down and choosing how long you want the Sleep Focus to be on before bed.

Before your planned sleep time, the Sleep Focus switches off the watch screen and activates Do Not Disturb.

Attempt one of the following:

Your schedule's days should be set: Then click Active On, then tap your schedule. Click days, then choose.

Change the time you get up and go to bed by tapping Schedule, selecting

Wake Up or Bedtime, setting a new time using the Digital Crown, and then tapping Check.

Set the alarm's parameters: Toggle Alarm on or off, then select an alarm sound by tapping Your Schedule, followed by Sound & Haptics.

Change Sleep Options

On your Apple Watch, launch the Settings application.

After selecting Sleep, change these options:

When you specify a wind down time in the Sleep app, the Sleep Focus automatically turns on at that time.

Switch off this option if you'd rather manage the Sleep Focus manually in Control Center.

Your iPhone's Lock Screen and Apple Watch interface have been streamlined for sleep mode to minimize distractions.

While the Sleep Focus is engaged, display the time and date on your iPhone and Apple Watch.

On or off switches for charging reminders and sleep tracking.

The health app on your iPhone receives sleep data when Sleep Tracking is enabled on your Apple Watch.

To have your Apple Watch prompt you to charge it before bedtime and to let you know when it is charged up, turn on Charging Reminders.

On your iPhone, you can also modify these sleep settings. On your iPhone, launch the Apple Watch app, select My Watch, and then select Sleep.

View Recent Sleep History

Get your Apple Watch and launch the Sleep application.

Browse to see the amount of sleep you got the previous night, how long you spent in each phase of sleep, and how much sleep you obtained on average over the previous 14 days.

Launch the Health application on your iPhone, select Explore, and select Sleep to see your iPhone's sleep history. Click Show More Sleep Data to get more information, such as the average amount of time you slept in each stage of sleep.

Review your sleeping respiratory rate

You can gain more understanding of your general health by using your Apple Watch to monitor your respiratory rate while you sleep. Once you've worn your watch to bed, take these actions:

On your iPhone, launch the Health app, select Browse, and then select Respiratory.

Select Show More Respiratory Rate Data after selecting Respiratory Rate.

The variation of your breathing rate while you slept is displayed in the Sleep entry.

Reminder: The measures of respiratory rate are not meant for medical purposes.

Chapter Five

Unlock Your Mac with Apple Watch

When your Mac wakes from sleep and is running macOS 10.13 or newer version, your Apple Watch will automatically open it. The same Apple ID must be used to log into iCloud on your Watch 8 and Mac.

The version year of your Mac can be found by selecting About This Mac from the Apple menu in the top-left corner of your computer monitor. The model number is followed by the year your Mac was produced, for as "MacBook Pro (15-inch, 2018)."

Activate Auto-Unlocking

Ensure the following settings are used on your devices:

On your Mac, Wi-Fi and Bluetooth is enabled.

The same Apple ID that you use to sign into iCloud on your Mac and Apple Watch is also enabled for two-factor verification.

You're using a passcode on your Watch 8.

Visit System Preferences under the Apple menu.

Choose General, then click Security & Privacy.

Choose "Unlock applications and your Mac using your Apple Watch."

Choose the Apple Watch you wish to utilize to open your applications and Mac if you have more than one.

If two-factor verification isn't enabled for your Apple ID, try checking the box once more after following the onscreen instructions.

Read Mail on Apple Series Watch

Read your email using your Watch 8 and respond utilizing QWERTY keyboard (not accessible in all languages, only for Apple Watch Series 7 and Apple Watch Series 8), scribble, dictation or emoji, or a ready reply. Alternatively, it could change to your iPhone and respond there.

read notifications for mail

Immediately increase your wrist when the notification appears to read a new message.

Move down from the top of the notification or click Dismiss at the message's conclusion to cancel it.

If you skip the message, click it when you next see unread alerts by swiping down on the watch face.

Launch the Apple Watch app on your iPhone, hit My Watch, then select Mail > Custom to manage email notifications.

Write And Reply to Mail on Apple Watch

Create a message

Open the Mail app on your Apple Watch 8.

After using the Digital Crown to move to the top of the screen, click new message.

To include a recipient, click Add Contact. To select an account to send from, click From. To include a subject line, click Add Subject. Finally, tap Create Message.

Compose a message

A message can be written in different ways, the majority of them on a screen. After tapping the Create Message icon, choose one or more of the following to do:

Use the QuickPath and QWERTY keyboards: Make use of the QuickPath keyboard to move from one letter to the next without having to raise your finger by tapping the characters to input them. Lift your finger to conclude a word.

As you type, recommended words emerge. Additionally, you can click a completed or incomplete word to highlight it and then flip the Digital Crown to view recommended texts. To submit the highlighted proposal, stop twisting the Digital Crown.

Move up from the down and press the Keyboard button if you can't see the keyboard.

Scribble: Write your message with your finger. Use the Digital Crown to place the cursor before making any edits to your message.

When making use of predictive text, simply click completed or incomplete text to emphasize it, then flip the Digital Crown to view recommended words. Stop twisting the Digital Crown to input the highlighted proposal, stop twisting the Digital Crown.

If you've configured your Watch 8 to use multiple languages, a separate language can be selected when using

Scribble. To select a language, simply move up from the bottom of the display.

Some languages do not have Scribble accessible.

Text to be dictated: Press the Dictate button, speak your message, and then press Done. Punctuation can also be spoken, as in "did it arrive question mark."

Switch the Digital Crown or hit the Scribble button to start using Scribble once more.

Emoji can be added by tapping the Emoji button, selecting a category or commonly used emoji at the bottom of the page, and then scrolling through the accessible pictures. When you locate the appropriate icon, click it to include it in your notification.

Input text with your iPhone: If your associated iPhone is close when you begin writing a message, a message on the iPhone will display suggesting allowing you input text through using iOS keyboard. On your iPhone, click the notification and then type the message.

Reply to a Message on Apple Watch

In the Mail app, move to the bottom of a notification you've gotten and select Reply. Tap Reply All if there are many recipients. After selecting Add Message, choose one of the following:

Send a wise response: You can send one of the helpful phrases from the list by tapping it. Scroll to see it.

Launch the Apple Watch application on your iPhone, press My Watch, select Mail > Default Replies, and then tap Add reply to add your own sentence. Click Edit, then move to rearrange them, or click the Delete button to remove one, to change the default responses.

If the intelligent responses are not available in the language you want, move bottom, select Languages, and then select a language. The languages you have activated on your iPhone under Settings > General > Keyboard > Keyboards are those that are accessible.

Write a response: After tapping the Add Message field, type your response.

Set Timers on Apple SERIES Watch

You can monitor time with the aid of the Timers app on Apple series Watch. Multiple timers that keep a track of time for close to 24 hours can be set.

Say something along the lines of "Set a timer for 1 hour," using Siri.

Set a timer immediately.

On your Apple series Watch, launch the Timers application.

Click a duration (such as 10, 15 or 20 minutes) or a timer that you have used before below Recents to start a timer quickly. Move down and click Custom to make a custom timer.

It is possible to hit the Repeat Timer button to initiate another timer with the same period when a timer expires.

Pause or End a timer

Visit the Timers app on your series Watch while a timer is set.

Click the Pause, Play, or End buttons to start, stop, or continue the action, respectively.

Make A Personalized Timer

On your Apple series Watch, launch the Timers application.

Tap Custom once you've reached top of the visuals.

To change, flip the Digital Crown and click on hours, minutes, or seconds.

Press Start.

Stopwatch

Open and select a stopwatch

If you've included a stopwatch or are using the Chronograph watch faces, tap the stopwatch on your watch face in order to access the Stopwatch app or launch it.

On the Stopwatch screen, select Analog, Digital, Graph, or Hybrid.

While looking at a stopwatch, click, then select a format to change the format.

Start, stop, and reset the stopwatch

Choose a format, launch the Stopwatch application on your Watch 8, and then carry out one of these actions:

To begin, press the Start button.

Take a lap: Press the Lap button.

Then finally, note: Press the Stop button.

Stop the stopwatch and press the Reset button to restart it.

Even if you return to the watch face or visit other apps, the timing keeps going.

Review results on the timing display.

Alarm

The Apple Watch's Alarms app should be opened.

Click Add Alarm.

Before selecting the hours or minutes, tap AM or PM.

When using 24-hour time, there is no need for this step.

After adjusting, turn the Digital Crown, press the Check button.

Tap the alarm's switch to switch it on or off. To configure repeat, or snooze options, you may also have to click on the alarm time.

Tip: Enable silent mode to make up an alarm that only requires you tapping your wrist, and which makes no noise.

Don't let yourself snooze

You can press Snooze to delay the next alarm for a while when an alarm is off. To prevent snooze, take the following actions:

the Apple Watch's Alarms app should be opened.

Toggle off Snooze by tapping the alarm from the listed alarms.

Skip A Wake-Up Alarm

Your iPhone's alarm should be set.

Launch the Apple series Watch app on your iPhone.

Press Clock, then My Watch, to enable Push Notifications from iPhone.

When an alarm echoes, your Apple series Watch notifies you so you can snooze or ignore the alarm. (When your Apple Watch alarms sound, your iPhone is not notified.)

Configure Apple series Watch to function as a nightstand alarm clock.

On your Apple series Watch, launch the Settings application.

Switch on to Nightstand Mode by going to General, then click on Nightstand Mode.

The period of any alarms has set, the date, then present time are all displayed when you plug your Watch into its charger and activate bedside mode.

Contacts

The Apple Watch's Contacts app should be opened.

To navigate your contacts, switch the digital crown.

To view details and notes for a contact, tap on them.

Communicate with contacts

Direct communication options include calling, texting, emailing, and starting a Walkie-Talkie through the Contacts app.

The Apple series Watch's Contacts app should be opened.

To navigate your contacts, switch the digital crown.

Do these after tapping a contact:

To view the contact's numbers, click the Phone icon. To dial a number, simply click it.

Open an already existing message thread or start a another one by tapping the Message button.

To compose an email, use the Email icon.

If a person has already received your invitation, tap the Walkie-Talkie icon to invite them again.

Create a Contact

The Apple series Watch's Contacts app should be opened.

Click New Contact after swiping downward.

Name the contact and, if applicable, company.

Click Add after entering your email, mobile number and address.

Share, edit or extract a contact

the Apple Watch's Contacts app should be opened.

To navigate your contacts, turn your digital crown.

Move down and click Share Contact, Edit Contact, or Delete Contact after tapping a contact.

Siri

Siri's useful commands

On the Apple series Watch, utilize Siri to carry out tasks and acquire information. For instance, Siri may translate your words into a different language, recognize a song and immediately give a clear Shazam result, or, in response to a broad enquiry, show the first few query results also, a little extract from each page. To access the page on Apple series Watch, simply press Open Page. Use Siri to perform tasks that would typically need you do a few things.

Not all countries or languages have Siri. View the watchOS feature availability article on your Apple assistant website.

Siri: Use a phrase like:

"How do you speak that in Chinese?"

How To Use Siri

The following actions will ask Siri for something:

Speak into your Apple series Watch by raising your wrist.

Visit the Settings application on your series Watch, click Siri, and then switch off Raise to Speak to disable the feature.

To give an order to order to Siri, simply say "Hey Siri," then give your order.

Launch the Settings app on your Apple series Watch, touch Siri, and then select "Hey Siri" to disable. Watch out for "Hey Siri."

Press the Siri button on your series
watch face.

Once the listening indication appears,
click and hold the Digital Crown while
speaking your request.

Launch the Settings app on your Apple
series Watch, hit Siri, and then select
Press Digital Crown to disable the Click
Digital Crown feature.

Respond to notifications with AirPods
and Beats headphones on your Apple
series Watch.

When you are using compatible AirPods
or Beats headphones, Siri can read out

messages from different applications without the need to open your iPhone. To be able to respond without saying "Hey Siri," Siri refrains from disturbing you and listens after reading notifications.

Turn on Announce Notifications

Dependent on the type of headphones you have, place the linked pair on your ears.

Connect them to your Watch 8.

On your Apple series watch, launch the Settings application.

Announce Notifications may be turned on by going to Siri > Announce Notifications.

On your iPhone, access your Settings app, select Notifications > Announce Notifications, and activate Announce Notifications.

Reply a message

Simply say, "Reply that's excellent news," for example.

Siri requests for confirmations after repeating whatever you must have said before proceeding to sending your response. (On your Watch 8, visit the

Settings application select Siri, then next, Announce Notifications, scroll to the bottom, then select Reply without Confirmation to go ahead and send replies without requesting confirmation.)

Choose Apps for Notifications

The applications that are permitted to notify on notifications are up to you.

Dependent on the type of headphones you have, place the linked pair on your ears.

On your Apple series Watch, launch the Settings application.

Scroll down then select the apps you wish to receive audio messages from after going to Siri > Announce Notifications.

Temporarily Turn Off Announce Notifications

To access Control Center, click and hold the downside of your screen, then swipe upward.

Select Announce Notifications from the menu.

To activate it, tap the Announce Notifications button one in repeated succession.

Whenever you take out your AirPods, the Announce Notifications button is disabled.

Watch Faces

The Watchface Gallery

The simplest way to view any watch face which is offered is done through the Face Gallery in the Apple series watch app. You may edit it, select complexities, and then add the face to your collection whenever you find one that looks intriguing—all from the gallery.

On your iPhone, launch the Apple Watch application, and select Face Gallery.

Pick features for the face.

Tap on a face in your Face Gallery, next, click a feature like color or whatever you prefer.

The top face changes as you experiment with various possibilities to enable your design to be excellent.

Add Complications to YOUR Face Gallery
Choose a face in the Face Gallery, next, click a position for the complications— for example, Top Left.

When complications are accessible for that point, swipe to reveal them, then click the exact one you prefer.

Navigate to the top of your list and click Off if you choose you do not want an issue at that spot.

Customizing the Apple Watchface

Create a customized Apple Watch face with the features you require and the appearance you choose. Select a design, alter the color and other details, and then include it in your collection. Change faces whenever necessary to get a presentation of the proper time tracking equipment or to stir things up.

The simplest method of seeing all of the watch faces that are offered is to have one personalized or customized and add it to your gallery is through the Face menu in the Apple series application. However, you can modify your watch face on your watch if your iPhone is not nearby.

Choose ANOTHER watch face

To view other watch faces in your gallery, navigate from one point to another across the dial.

Press and hold onto the watch face, then move to the exact one you choose, then click it to show all your watch faces that are accessible.

You can add Complications to the Apple Watch series Face

Workout

Start Training

Get your Apple Watch's Workout application open.

You should switch the Digital Crown to the desired exercise.

Select Add Workout at the bottom of your screen for workouts like kickboxing or surfing. .

Click the workout when you are sure that you want to start.

Your selections are reflected in the sequence of the workouts as you use your applications and select them.

Visit the Apple Support page About Workout Types to get more information on the many workouts you can perform with the Apple series watch.

Siri: Use a phrase like:

"Begin your 30-minute run."

"Walk for five miles."

"Begin your 300-calorie bike ride

Voiceover

Turn Voiceover On/Off

On your Apple series, launch the Settings application.

VoiceOver can be activated by going to Accessibility > VoiceOver.

Also, double tap on the VoiceOver button to switch it off.

VoiceOver can also be switched on or off by using Siri.

You may also activate VoiceOver for your Apple series on your iPhone by opening your watch application on your phone, selecting My Watch, going to Accessibility, and then selecting VoiceOver. Alternately, you can use your accessibility shortcut path.

Voiceover Gestures

In order to operate your Apple series 8 with VoiceOver, use these gestures.

Keep in mind: The Always On Display is supported by VoiceOver. VoiceOver concentrates on the element that you are to tap on the dimmed display when you do so.

Explore the screen: Hearing the name of each thing you touch as you move your finger across the screen can be enabled. Additionally, moving right or left is enabled by using a finger to choose an object that is nearby or click an item to select it. To view additional pages, use your two fingers to swipe to any direction that you desire, whether up or down.

Go back: Use your two fingers to create a "z" shape on your display screen to see if you've taken a turn you weren't expecting.

Act on an item: You will need to use a double click to open an app, change an option, or carry out any other operation when VoiceOver is activated. Tap on select a list item, app icon, or option switch, then double tap the selected item to carry out the action. For instance, choose the VoiceOver button, then double click anywhere around the display screen to disable VoiceOver.

Perform additional actions: When choosing an item, go ahead to pay vivid attention to the words "actions available" as some things offer many actions. Double tap after selecting an action with your icon used to swipe up or down.

Pause reading: Use your two fingers to click the display to stop VoiceOver from reading. To continue, go ahead to tap with your two fingers once more.

Adjust VoiceOver volume: Slide either up or down after twice tapping and holding with your two fingers. Alternately, launch the Apple series watch application in your iPhone, click on My Watch, then select VoiceOver under Accessibility.